Doctors Discover What Makes You Sick

Branca Tani

Rosen REAL READERS

Rosen Classroom™
New York

When you get sick, you are likely to go to the doctor.

Doctors go to school for a long time. They know a lot about the body.

When you visit the doctor, he or she will ask you questions. Your doctor wants to find out why you are sick.

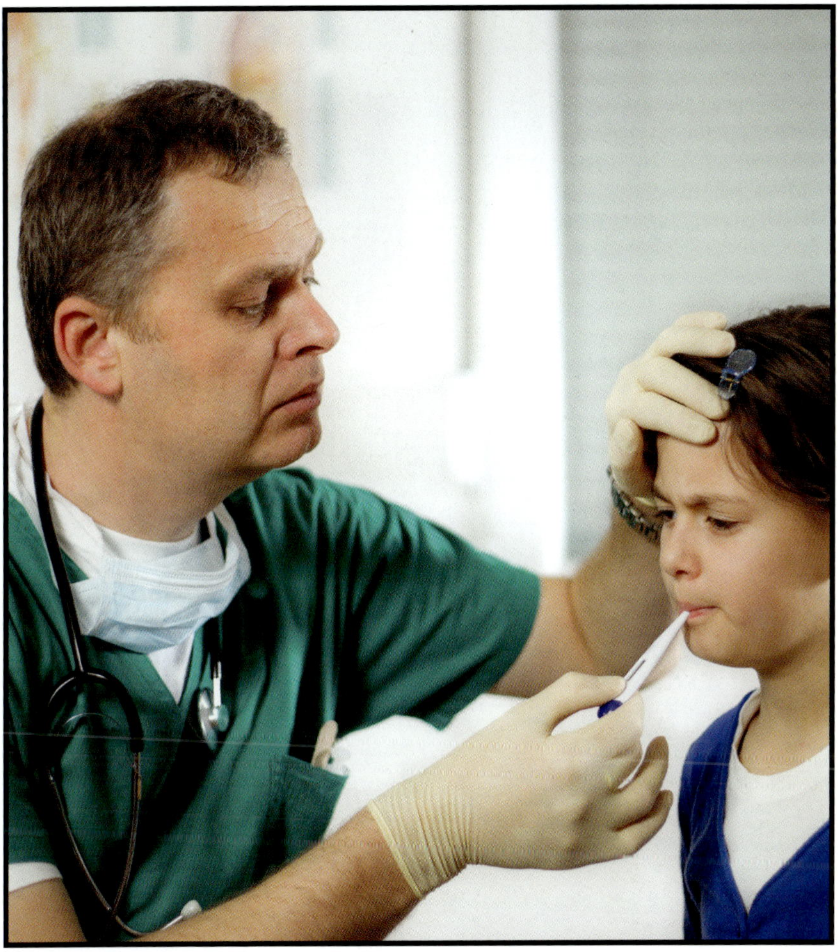

The doctor uses tools to help him.
He will check your temperature.
Do you have a fever?

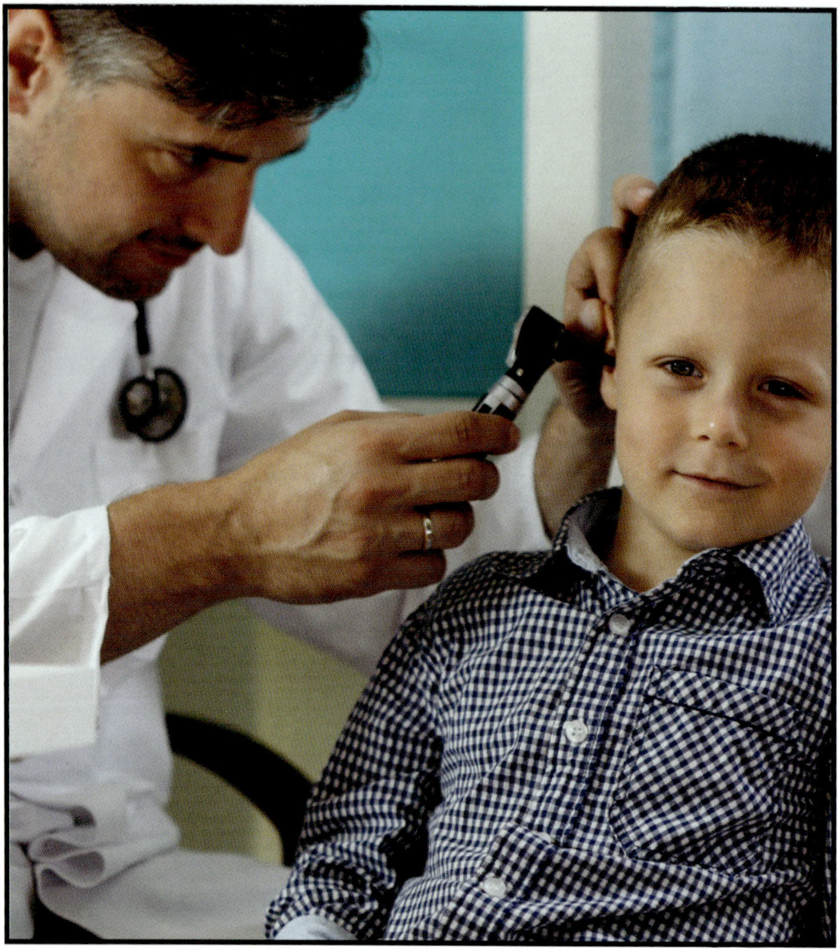

Special lights allow the doctor to check your ears, nose, and throat. Do you have a cold?

A doctor listens to your breathing. She listens to your heartbeat, too. She is looking for clues about why you are sick.

If your throat is red, a doctor may rub it with a cotton swab. She will send it to a lab for tests. You might have strep throat.

Maybe you have a rash or a stomachache. The doctor may ask what you have been eating. You could have an allergy. The doctor is still looking for clues.

The doctor is done with his exam. He will tell you what he thinks is making you sick. He will tell you what to do to feel better.

Doctors discover what makes you sick. They help your body feel better, too. That is their job!

Words to Know

doctor

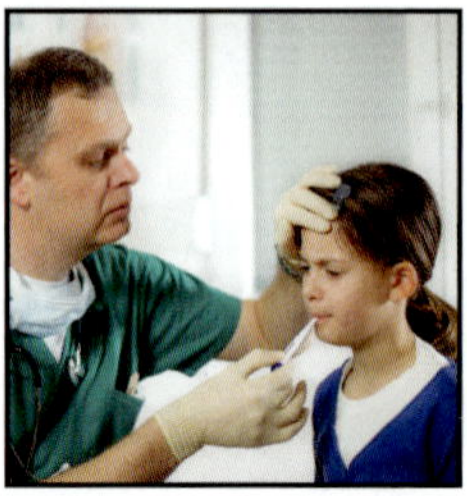

temperature

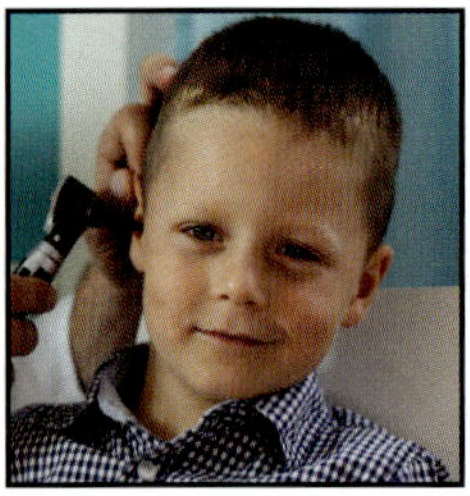

ears

heartbeat

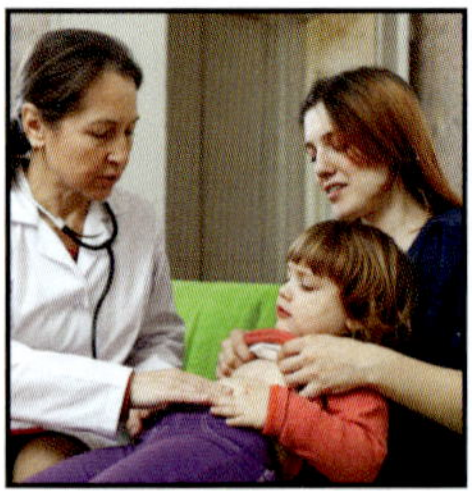

stomachache